MAUNDER

MAUNDER

Claire Kelly

Palimpsest Press
1171 Eastlawn Ave.
Windsor, Ontario. N8S 3J1
www.palimpsestpress.ca

Book and cover design by Dawn Kresan. Typeset in Adobe Garamond Pro, and printed offset on Rolland Zephyr Laid at Coach House Printing in Ontario, Canada. Edited by Dawn Kresan.

Palimpsest Press would like to thank the Canada Council for the Arts, and the Ontario Arts Council for their support of our publishing program. We also acknowledge the assistance of the Government of Ontario through the Ontario Book Publishing Tax Credit.

Library and Archives Canada Cataloguing in Publication

Kelly, Claire, 1984–, author
         Maunder / Claire Kelly.

Poems.
Issued in print and electronic formats.
ISBN 978-1-926794-38-9 (softcover)
ISBN 978-1-926794-45-7 (PDF)

         I. TITLE.

PS8621.E5587M38 2017   C811'.6   C2016-908118-4
                                       C2016-908119-2

For Rob

CONTENTS

Waiting
because where can a girl go
at midnight in small town Canada
with her head full of tadpoles?

—TAMMY ARMSTRONG

Your First Love, a Vacant Siding

Growing up trestle-struck
every day you walk the tracks
in the industrial part of town.
Factories steam-run
like trains.
          Film noir shortcut
from the stores to your apartment
where the winter-sewers plume.

Picnic tables almost to the track,
warehouse workers
                 smoking and leering.
You get stared at for walking in this place
unless you've got a lit cigarette.

You want to find the main line running north
and keep going
          until winter turns
to spring, until the flood melt
seeps
     up to the rails.
The rain refusing to stop.
An absurd amount of water,
the ground can't hold.

The trees study the situation:
the woods filled with water,
the trees and you reflected, doubled,
the grey sky
         the grey water.
The track the only thing single.

The Observer Effect

The observer effect refers to changes in a subject's behavior caused by an awareness of being observed.
　　　　　　　　　　　—DENNIS COON and JOHN MITTERER,
　　　　　　　　　　　from *Psychology: A Journey*

I

After placing makeshift daisy
chains atop our heads, we burnish
our parchment throats golden
with buttercups. Chalky palms
smudge dock leaves, subtle
markers we're led to after
nettle-sting. That the salve
grows near the bite feels
tantamount to proof. Though
the real lesson is that we both
dye and are dyed by the world.

II

In pond-beds the tadpoles
are gone, having grown foot-wise
and warted. Limbs and flawed skin
like lessons learned. These
lessons are flies tongue-snapped
from mid-air or croaks warning
danger's nearby or is here now,
is us studying steep banks
and the root systems of bulrushes
and cattails looking for signs
of erosion under our boots.

III

Remember tall grass stamped
flat as desktops. How thermoses
brimmed with dandelion wine.
How among poppies we reclined,
fingers carelessly strumming
the spindly stems of less
vibrant wildflowers—Snowdrops,
Bachelor's Buttons, Toothworts.
How after disturbing and being
disturbed by fire ants
we moved on.

Keeping Track, Keeping Pace

I. SWAGGER

The way sparse hips attune themselves
after a day spent
                perched on a barstool
    or a loyal horse.

A paradox: it's taking time,
measuring it out
                in prolonged strides,
        but it's also a tear to the target,
a dogged drumbeat in the mind. Spittoon-twang,   bull's eye.

No, it's not smooth, it's
rhythmic:
                John Wayne advertising adventure wholesale
                with its tricky fine print of encroachment, isolation,
                and—*awr, shucks*—sex.

Muscles slackened, overtasked,
the bone framework bearing everything up,
        almost lurching

                but fluid.
The slightly bowed legs,
                swinging. Grass blades bent
        in subtle arcs. Grit scuffed against
floorboards.

The extra effort it takes
to propel forward at a slower, cooler pace.

II. SHUFFLE

An unsound edifice,
  not teetering,
      but only because no one wants
to risk life, limb, and neck.

  Catastrophe is possible
      even when
there's a lack of exertion.

  The buses line up like cherries
      in a slot machine,
one in each window.
    Riders trickling out
        like grimy jackpot coins.

Here's an army of slouch and grimace.
  If the floors weren't mopped,
      kicked-up dust
would silt the lungs.

  There's talk of luck—good and bad—
      and of timing.
Timing's everything.

  Man, it's always a gamble
      even when you refuse to play.

III. PROMENADE

Vertigo between the metal beams.
      The earth nudged crooked,
axis tipping with each footfall.

      Keep the horizon level.
Point at it with your chin.
      Narrow your focal point to the furthest girder.

Enmeshed around the lights, thick-abdomened
      spiders. Ignore how they're harnessed
in while you're free to plummet.

      Pretend you're deaf to the rowdy wind.
Pretend your partner is a stable
      influence: hook arms and match pace.

It's not love that brings you here—
      out over the water—though
there's something to be said

      for the sound of bike treads
rolling along weathered planks,
      that bracing pulse

like a runner's heart pushing past the point
      of exertion and her
still going. But if you fell,

for an instant, broken surface tension
would envelop like an aura,
     holding you safe in light-drenched shallows.

IV. LURCH AND REEL

A teetering tin-can man coerces his creaky bike.
Seven-o'clock shadowed, jaundiced,
          and with a basket
full of cans to be returned, he's himself

until he swerves
          thumping over a gutter grate,
     slamming static.
                    Stillness transforms him, gives an earned grace,
          his skinny leg perched on the curb like a wading bird's.

     Although nothing's happened,
     you think you hear the tin and glass clatter:
                    a morning's work spilled on the bike lane.
                              But instead, the picker
pushes off and away,

                    and you stutter-step on too
shadowing some off-kilter scent,

          noticing a banded snake—aquamarine and ash—
     that's actually
                    just a skinny branch fallen,
crooked by wind,   lichen plastered.

     And to the left, a Lab mouth-cracking
                         a plastic bottle. A tethered threat.
          Piecemeal domestication.   Globs of spit coating
     a daydream of bones and marrow.

V. HOBBLE

i)

a pebble clatters in   the hollow sole of
a rubber boot
   erratic,   spasmodic rhythm:
                crimson marionette with
a snagged string

   forget the   sweet william plots on either side—
              oh,
     prissy evenness
the horizon swelling and   receding, sloping,
    jostling: this
    corrupted   vertigo world

ii)

pockmarked, a ball bearing   pelted by acid rain
                  a joint
    seized
      the ache of immobility   the pivot
     elsewhere, exaggerated   misdirection without deception

     Chaplin hesitates   to doff a bowler
   shuffles, shifts
all movement to his cane,   a supple swoop

 this endurance of uneasy
         movement   earns the limelight

VI. STRUT

Cluster poise and cluster pose

but in movement.

My muses of trend and style,

their intriguing structural sway, lovely.

Here in Mazucca's Lane

there's time to consider

impact, length of leg.

Fabric shifting in swells.

Possibility of skin.

The lighting's gotta be perfect.

Strobe. Muybridge sequence:

a horse galloping. In slow-mo.

Four Seasons on the Bus: Spring

The spring lamb's turned feral, violent. Won't be sheered.
I ask, *What'd you learn today?* He bares his teeth:
Grr! Spells it out GEE ARR ARR. Titters bitterly
as the tulips jab through cool soil and again
when the frost returns to shrivel their petals. Always cheering
for ice jams, he can't help but want every covered bridge
to spin half-submerged downriver into the next, a domino-
effect that'll push the province further into the red, that'll end
the seasonal migration of travellers rubbernecking maritime
kitsch with a fervour he just doesn't get. His favourite colour
is usually orange, sometimes black. But he likes anything
that clashes: plaid and stripes, Samoan-punk with bagpipes.
Soon he buzzes a 90's fade. Buzzes *FUCK OFF!*
on the side of his bullet head. Tries to hide his grin
when geriatrics in the third-best mall in town are shocked.
Takes to wearing a leather jacket, carrying a switchblade.
But it's all performance; he bawls most days.
Can see the fences being built around him.
Is sure the sun rising earlier each morning
has a common-sense plan that he can't say no to.

Apollo in a Sulky

Behind a row of stark ashes, a harness racer
practices laps, circles the track at a middling
pace, wheels kicking up scant waves of wet
snow at the turns.
                    To push through too-
bracing wind without the comfort of riding on
a horse as its muscles jolt like sparks
from tinder;
                    it's beyond me, this art of
hobbies, up-at-dawns, checking hooves and
wiping down flanks before they turn
to chill.
            Though I'm close enough to steam
the pane, I don't even watch until my tea
cools. Won't open the window to hear the
galumphing rhythm of his horse
orbiting orbiting
                    at a speed that shames
the winter sun that's hiding under a down
comforter of cloud—like how I,
taking the emblematic blanket for my own,
will soon be doing in my curtain-
dimmed room.
                    So I turn my back to his canter,
not wanting to see him stop, but to picture him
catching a gust that froths him aloft,
higher higher
                    dispelling the clouds, sun-pricking
the snow to near-blinding glint.

Honing in the Too-early Morning

Your mouth coils cigarette smoke
that trellises up, catches in the umbrella's canopy.
As in a house fire, it's best to avoid
the exposed beams: the lower air
is safer, rain so soft it's a heavy mist
that permeates and drenches as if by thought
more than contact or diffusion. The Saint John,
a steal slough, chains the city's torso.
You adore this river the way an escape artist
cherishes a key, want to keep it
tucked away in a fold of skin
in your inner cheek. But here the water's

too polluted for gulping, even accidentally,
so you think of propelling from it like *tah-dah*
and take your bows beside the steep banks,
a cat-like assistant in a rhinestone bustier
holding her arm out towards you
in mock awe. Relief unspools down the sidewalk.
While in the eastern sky, a crimson threat
retreats to muted clouds. Return,
return to another unruffled morning,
to home, the oh-so-friable calm
between foghorn blasts. My body
in procession is bracketed

by the hallway: will you dream
of here when gone far away?
Let us live like Labs do. Dig
in the garden for the sake of digging

in the garden. Tear the neon green felt
from tennis balls. And whine for our supper
if it's late—tragicomic hunger
stuck in the ever-panting present
'til we howl like a pack missing us. Oh,
a guitar pick is the distance between you
and sound. If you give up your hard-earned
callouses, we might be lost.

As if you steeped and drank these streets

Gravelly cement, unswept after winter.
Shoes scraping. Thoughts needing to
grind against something too.
                            This week
a season of scents unfroze, and the
leashed dogs, all a-flurry, pulled one way,
then another. Their collars tugging tight,
they orbited their owners: all nose, all
animal glee.
                    But these March thoughts
loosen like scarves that are more
decorative than necessary. These mild
opiate evenings getting longer. These dusk
dreams.
                At a driveway's end, a cat
distractedly shifts as I beckon it, until from
underneath its squat and awkward form,
a mouse
                bolts towards the street and the cat,
made sleek by pursuit, follows a bound
behind.
                Both are in the near lane when the
pickup truck approaches like a plot point
promising climax. Then it turns.
                                    That's how
daily drama is avoided, with the monotonous
tick-tick-tick of a turn signal.

Reading Alden Nowlan's "Hens" at the Laundromat

The hens have already picked the old rooster dead
when I notice the priest tumbling his robes into
the washer.
          Dark shirt with the dog collar missing—
square of pallid skin under his Adam's apple.
                              He half-
reads a newspaper, glances up at the bulky, cast-off
TV, pops a piece of gum from a foil packet, palms it
into his mouth.
          An aroma of muddled detergent brands,
acrid bleach—his black and purple vestments jostling
in soapy water.
          Before this wash cycle did they smell
of incense—sandalwood, lemongrass, myrrh—or
of trapped cigarette smoke, rank cologne, spilled
wine, sweat?
          The others—a chick's brothers and sisters—
will always gather to peck the odd one into a mass of
bloody down.
          I pile my wet laundry into a wicker
hamper to hang at home.
          The priest massages his jaw,
tears a piece from the newspaper, spits out his chewed
wad, balls it up, and turns to the sports section.

Stumped by a Squat Frame

Every house I passed I tried to love
even the one painted garish colours:
tartish bruise of a door, acid-reflux
green of a window frame. And the one
with drain pipes angled like broken limbs,
ramshackle decrepitude, depression:
a retriever chained to a cinder block
hoarsely barking in mad boredom.

Campus workers mow new grass,
spread shredded cedar
around shrubs and tulip clusters.

A young man weedwacks too close
to an ancient elm, snaps the string.
He bends down on one knee—
a proposing posture—holds
the machine across his thigh to fix it,
swivelling the cap and unravelling
more twine. With the pieces back together,
he starts his racket up again
but forgets to finish the tree. Tall grass
half-hewn like a hem mis-sewn.
Stitches come undone. Fabric drooping.

That elm I adore
for all its awkwardness:
a geezer's technicolor

suspenders, plaid pants bisecting
a hard beer belly.
Forgiving it the way
I won't forgive the houses.

Two Days, Years Apart, Cézanne Caught a Storm

In response to Cézanne's painting:
Pyramid of Skulls, 1901,
and his death, 1906

Still-life tableaux
of stilled life,
human anatomy
arranged on the counter
like apples.

His housekeeper
rubbed his arms and legs
until he regained consciousness.

Four skulls in a pile,
the jawbones missing,
one head's concave sockets
titled to the ceiling.
tilted

When he fainted
on the second day
his model screamed.

Secret cache of a
gravedigger, madman.

A momento mori,
he was put to bed
and never left it.

You Arrive by Water

You arrive by water,
dragging your birch canoe
up a beach grown shallower
with each season.

A lake scrubbed clean.
Invaded. Mollusk-ridden.
We've been told to wear water
shoes before stepping in, but you
hop from the boat barefooted
like someone who's never been cut.

While you were gone, I dreamt
you had webbed toes, could talk with gulls
and terns, that you knew the mischief of otters.

As you stood on the cusp of the porch,
you clutched an omen, a goat willow branch,
its downy points cluttered with catkins, an early sign of melt.
You must have saved it for months, I thought,
preserving its windblown luck.

You told me
fragility conjures but should not be handled:
the fronds of a fern unfurling,
the symmetry of a glass sponge,
the gills of a mushroom.

And then I understood that for you
distance is learnt by touch.
Your name spoken into the space
between your shoulder blades.
The impartiality of water,
tides leaving, returning.

Street Haunting

Now when I walk around at lunchtime
I have only two charms in my pocket
—FRANK O'HARA

Downtown intersection of wool gathering
and window shopping.
                    Erratic steps, clipped
dodges. Collision being
            the true failure to connect.
                              An inner walk gone wrong:
my mind, a gymnast's spiralling ribbon,
                something loose and beautiful about
the planned   lack of plan,
as if, here, the only message is to maunder.

                    Reflection in a Ford's windscreen,
a public servant checks for fly-away hair
            then rejoins the foot traffic,

sidestepping
            a panhandler—NEED A JOB, PLEASE HELP!—

                coins jangling in a Tim's cup,
garbage bags wrapping his legs;
            they've called
                        for rain this afternoon.

I bypass him   to compare
            prices for things I'll never buy, thinking,
Let's choose the pearls; life could be changed.

And suddenly, I feel wily
as ivy up brickwork—the pavement
swooping vertical and I'm climbing,

half a mind on clefts in the sidewalk,
other half on thin air,

so it's all I can do to remember
how far home is from here.

First Hot Day

I find a pacifier on the asphalt,
nearly step on it, pastel mouth-stopper,
bulbous plug. Alien in shape
but not streamlined.
The colour of bubble gum
not yet trodden on.

My thighs, pale in wrinkled shorts,
are too root vegetable, pulpy
and solid. All around me
everything's showing off.
The breeze participates. The flowers,
such prima donnas, swirl like second
graders in first communion dresses.

A neighbour drags a wood-backed chair
out to the driveway, suns herself,
propping her legs along a cement barrier.
Her hair's pulled in a bun, toes pointing
to avoid an awkward tan.
A lazy ballerina, like us
she has no balcony or backyard,
but she makes do.

Our streets are full of friendly cats.
I pet them, unafraid of domesticated teeth,
of fleas, of being followed home.
One with peachy cheeks, a white chin,
half-grown and gangly, sprawls on the sidewalk.
Displays softness. Spring,
nothing but soft, desperate bellies.

Four Seasons on the Bus: Summer

The summer flowers chinwag
in groups of three or more.
Their voices bolting up and over
each other's like wayward
honeybees that've lost
their hives on purpose
and won't come down
to earth.

All winter and spring
they've been tightening
their petals: lunges, crunches,
push-ups, squats. And there's
not an inch they've not
analyzed for flaws.

On each of their geometric
laps sits a wicker bag that's
crammed with scented
sunscreen, bottled water,
pristine magazines, covers
squealing: Think success =
happiness? *Girl, you deserve
a VACAY!*

But now chlorine's bloomed
their eyes pot-head red,
and their tightly tied-back hair's
so desiccated, they're haloed
by tawny fly-aways, blossom-
shards coarsely torn like daisies
post-I-love-you-or-not.

When alone they reflect
that too much sun and time's
a pity, that they're tanned
as exhumed mummies. That it
used to be easier.

But in their bouquets
they still feel sexy-safe.
Even tough. Like strands
of gossamer twisted into
a garrotter's cord. Sometimes
they even forget to be bored.

And when they cease giggling,
they face everyone down
through the dual solar-eclipse
of their sunglasses, noses
pinched like the world's
just so much manure
that they must push
through.

All day *they can't even*,
they are *so over it*. And
all they can do is curl
their legs underneath
their sundress hems—
protective as bud-sheaths—
certain they'll soon be plucked.

Peony

Quand nous sommes très méchants, que ferait-on de nous?
When we are very bad, what would they do to us?
—ARTHUR RIMBAUD

It's hard to tell
who's in charge
of peony and ant's
symbiotic economy.

In myth, peony's
pure loner-genius,
scraper with a scalpel,
healing mortals
and demi-gods alike.

'Til his teachers
question their callings
and plot his death
and the gods deign

to free him
from his betters'
bloodletting ways.

Lazy peony basking,
secure in loamy earth.

Metamorphosed
from doctor to decoration.
Tightly packed atom of pre-flower,
can't burst open alone

So it's up to the ants
to do the dirty work,
dissecting, discerning
what to leave on the stalk.
Their mandibles picking away
at nectar-coated green.

Such tiny plastic
surgeons exposing beauty:
a lush blush firework,
a taffeta abundance.

The gods saving, condemning.
Petty planners.
Bitter children of divorce
dropping matches, spitting
from balconies.

For them peony is
a mere game gone awry,
a lesson:

only heal those you can control,
always make the payments steep.

Vultures over Cottage Country

Cycle of weeping light!
That mice and birds will eat you,
And you will spoil their stomachs
As you have spoiled my mind.
—LOUISE BOGAN

Airborne turkey vultures lurch
    like drunks hauled out of coupés.

        Their wormy heads
            are wholly foul, yet

               these buzzards digest what we can't.
                 Our mammalian ancestors knew

                     the vice-grip, the scoop
                     and terror, the talon slice.

                     Wingspan silhouettes
                propelling along savannah grass

            are the reason we search for patterns,
       even when there are none to be found.

        Above, two birds skate the sky
        with weak ankles.

     Reclining, we swat at mosquitoes,
sun-glare cuffs shut our eyes.

How to Survive a Bear Attack
(FOUND POEM)

For a second, I thought
I was dead.

That's the first thing
that comes to mind
when you open your eyes and
see that friggin' mouth full of teeth
and a tongue in there.

When I opened up my eyes
it was on top of me—
with the friggin' noise,
it's crazy the way
it growls. Not
from the mouth,
but right from
the stomach. So

last thing I remember
I had his tongue
in my hand.

I didn't want to let go
because he was tryin'
to fight me off.

And I says, *If you're goin'
to hurt me, I'm goin'
to hurt you too.* So

I hold on to him
and he's biting his tongue
at the same time
as tryin' to bite me.

What else could I grab?
You can't fight
a bear fair.

Gathering in the Parking Lot

Seagulls huddle like juvenile thugs.
All gullet and hunched shoulders,
they appear to have pocketed
everything within reach.

These petite actors manipulate space,
shrinking the world around them
so they loom.

A petulant cluster of un-sprung springs;
stillness promising action.

It is as if they could solve
all mechanical problems
            (unclogging drains, popping
            tricky corks, propelling high-speed
            trains along magnetic tracks)
if they cared to.

Only their calls sound distraught—
a screech of hollow hunger.

We met midway up the hill

as though grass blades were jury members we had to sway

as though the nighthawk's electronic chirps foretold an early frost

as though I might snatch a clump of moss, dry it for burning

as though marigolds smelled sweet, honey placards in civic planters

as though my screwball aunt cluttered the city streets with hobbyhorses

as though you ran naked through the library

as though I collapsed in a storm drain with all the hoodwinks I could
    muster

as though pennies took up copper arms

as though gears and chains learned to laugh

as though cars sung operettas

as though snares took to weaving themselves into bondage sweaters

as though we grew downy and professed love with carnivores, their
    clammy, serrated mouths

as though the whirligig spun for you alone and stilled when I breathed
    in its direction

Crows—fire-eaters

of the Trans-Can—strut
like off-duty pallbearers,
professional mourners
on a smoke break.

When I blink, I'm sure
they whip out flasks,
light menthols from
back-up packs.

Comfortable in their
death-knell stares,
while wearing dress-
shoes that pinch,
they crack jokes,

gallows-style (*What
d'you get a dead baby
for Christmas? Why can't
orphans play baseball?*)
as if to keep from crying
out, though at times

they can't help themselves,
their ember-charred throats
calling: *The show must go on.
The show must go on.*

The Human Gyroscope: A Study of Momentum

Olive Oyl swings and capers
in front of the bar band.
All sinew and bowl cut, zombie arms,
graceless angles. Plumpness on her
would be a joke: champagne thrown in the sea.

Her Popeye hunches his shoulders—
no can of spinach to be wolfed, just a bottle
of domestic—and observes his feet as if they plot
instead of plod.

Olive's whirligigging. Small breasts jostling
under flimsy fabric. She's
sped beyond   to another dimension,
(or has discovered dimensionless-ness).
                    She's a wild quark, a string theory jiving.
                    Broken loose, she's neither particle
                    nor wave. Something different.
                    The opposite of inert. A gas that might
                    spark more than mockery.

Cacophony. The drummer's over-the-top slaughter
of his rack-mounted toms ends the set.
It's all intake and outtake now.

Matter collapses into chairs.
Bathroom driven, Popeye pukes
all the way up the stairs and round the bend,
followed by an acolyte of bucket and mop
collecting another sample to be analyzed.

Ears ring with absence of racket.
Olive Oyl downs her whisky and soda.

Sole-worn Glass

Following twilight
appetites, he swallowed
unthinking the aphrodisiac
rumour of moths
        —CATHERINE GREENWOOD

Following twilight,
slight darkness,
then the girth of moonless black,
the charmless distance of footfalls,
pacing his own block as if it were new,
the world shrunk to the streetlights'
domed shrouds of brightness
that ask nothing but everything
of eyes, casting flickering
shadows that join, forgive, fight.
Before following twilight

appetites, he'd swallowed
a tumbler's worth of amber whisky,
decided to forgo food, instead
waded risky from that dim pub
to swelter the summer humidity
outside. Released from borrowed
barstool freedom, his slickened skin
his late-night musk, he almost
wished he was followed.
The appetites he swallowed

unthinkingly, the aphrodisiac
ampitheatre of crickets,
the broken glass under-shoe
so much less than shards:
glistening sand particles
of sole-worn glass. He reacts
as though propelled away
from himself; the haunting
of his double, a twin zodiac
unthinking the aphrodisiac

rumour of moths,
the rumour of months of stifled
breath against scarves, still remembers
the utter outline winter creates
between skin and wind-chilled open air,
unable to forget trapped vapour,
his own breath, the binding of cloth.
Though now, in contrast, he feels naked
and lighter, like he could step up,
fly off with the brittle hot
rumour of moths.

curb' *N.*—

A silver-plated Venetian penknife.

A blind woman's quilting needle.

A hockey stick blade overly bent and technically illegal.

A person who nods.

A chunk cut from the ear of a feral cat.

An albino python stuffed and mounted above a mantle.

The taste of under-ripe but still palatable fruit.

A photo of near-deathbed relatives.

A scar that brings hypnotic comfort.

The artistry between nudity and nakedness.

A prophesy from one unaccustomed to giving good news.

An ever-sullen Irishman.

Poem for a Busy Lover

Meet me at the beach
not sun-dappled but office pale
from coordinating schedules
with influential people,
your cyber rolodex
full as a toddler on Halloween.

No, meet me on the corner
of Queen and York at 5p.m.
when the sidewalks itch
with civic workers who have
no shortcuts over the construction-clogged
bridge, whose true desire paths
would lead them southward
to join the bootleg trails
of some American wilds
where outlaw ballads have told them
true freedom lives.

No. Simply meet me at home.
Keep elaborate plans
for those you must impress,
those balloon confrères
so easily inflated,
their latex heads banging
along ceiling tiles
'til their helium brains
leak out.

At home we can submerge
like pygmy hippos, rotund
and buoyant. Or fold
imprecisely and lazily
like flannel sheets in August,
crammed right at the back
of the linen cupboard.

We can be two cans
lined up and shot off
a wooden fence
that miraculously
fall and settle
next to each other,
damaged, yet somehow
safe, even serene.

Four Seasons on the Bus: Fall

The fall term holds onto the pole,
but barely. She's forgotten her keys,
her wallet, her backpack. Someone
should have seen to her needs:
burnt back the summer-dry
stubble, dragged her chockablock
cornucopia straight to class.

In the only open seat, she lands
like a brassy laugh at a funeral.
Across the aisle a prophetic
five-year-old boy—wizened,
like he's been up reading Nietzsche
by flashlight—expounds: *No gorillas
on the bus! No gorillas on the bus!
Only monkeys in the cars!* But what

does that mean? She's left her notes!
Or lost them! Or never made any!
It's all collapsed, the boy's father's
reedy face, exhaustion. Her scarf
is an upside-down exclamation mark,
her head the floating point. *How long,*
she pleads, *until Thanksgiving break?*
She's still got time to learn something.

Before the Dream in which She is Followed Begins

Take this angular threat, a man
with heavy shoes. Her forehead swarms
in the wind she can't tell him what she wants,
doesn't want to. She is not a complex knot for him to sever.

He is not a knight's singing blade,
but a Tom Sawyer penknife that sticks and needs oiling.

She thinks but doesn't say,
Stranger, I don't want to hear what son-in-law luck led you
out past the dooryard with too-red lips, windshorn, burnt.

He says,
My own love is grey-mottled, lame
my seagull love cries out and struts the parking lot
my seagull belly is never quite as full
my seagull timepiece is always calling out the hour
when it is not the hour, its strap pinches!

The man with heavy shoes kicks heavily,
this guy with his sidewalk-echo and his ever-
hankering to be somewhere else, maybe where she is,
pushing at or through like a drill bit.

And soon, as needs must, she is half a block ahead
and hastening, her shoes feathery,
quiet as a whispered shibboleth…

As an October caterpillar is late,

so do my thoughts frost themselves
to pavement. A man walks towards me

humming *Sweet Caroline*, his big toe peering
through a canvas shoe. Let his body pull apart

other seams. Tear out the train tracks. Cut
the long leads of dogs so they can dash about

in the dead grass. Cut any thoughts I had of pathways
or trade winds, dull the gusts of my daylight hours,

make them flat as dusk lake-tops.
As if sensing his ability to dismantle, he quiets,

crushes his smoked-to-the-stub Pall Mall,
and steps onto the bus that will take him

to the northside, the doors shuttering
and the bus chuffing like a sleep apnea

machine, over the bridge to an almost other town.

I Dreamt I Could Fly; I Awoke Encased in Lead.

All's fair choked the blackbird, my bird-tongue,
my feathered hollow-boned idea. Flight is predictable
but sour when it fails. I worked like a gnome
into the night; by morning no one believed in me.
I am sure the worm knew something, arriving earlier
and earlier, safe in the pre-dawn. My shadow thins.
The crows shriek a dreadful din in the hedgerow. A turkey vulture
wheels overhead, tilting in the breeze, awkward and ominous.
Its sunburnt head and wrinkled flesh should be laughable.
They can smell the dead—and the long dying—across county lines.
They are welded to the food chain like weights. I see one,
but its mate must be near, circling me as I sink. Did I really
used to think the dead floated safe from clutching weeds?

Shield Lichen

You say Ovid's gods transformed
Miss Havisham into a lanky oak,
and her wedding dress sprang up fungal.

The lace stiffened with age.
The bodice frayed
where her vinegar tears fell.

A veil of pollen
she only remembers in springtime.

You say the gods
can be real bastards,
though they know of beauty
that needs stillness and damp.
They know loss
immortal.

But how can she be
so lonely now?
Her garments grown
into another skin, a living thing.

And her home—neither lost
nor reclaimed—ripened into
a poplar copse around her.

This Hefty Wadding

Eaves trough. Tin roof. Rain
tapping staccato. A widow's walk
on my shoulder. Gun-metal grey
staircase corkscrewing from right hip,
angling up my torso to collar bone.
When I breathe the steps shake
like an old footbridge in a windstorm.

I have been building a nest that is my body,
layering homespun blankets with high
thread counts. Enticing cloth, but protective,
bullet-and-shank-proof, eye-proof.
Laying fabrics the way priests lay hands.

Things stick to me.
A comb missing six prongs.
A dented hubcap. Enough pennies
for a cup of tea. A two-year-old
lotto ticket, the numbers faded. Ribbon,
string, newspaper pulped in the snow.
An old mitten, thumbless. A detached
suitcase handle.

Thinking me slow, joggers speed past.
They don't see my vigour,
the tense architecture of my thighs,
how heavy a nest can be.

Similes from Pure Sleep

Linguistically, sleep loss appears to interfere with novel
responses and the ability to suppress routine answers.
— YVONNE HARRISON and JAMES HORNE,
from *The Journal of Sleep Research*

Stubborn as a turntable
spinning Wu-Tang Clan
until the neighbours pound
an aggrieved beat
on the 3a.m. walls.

Jagged as the schismatic end
of a too-close friendship,
with hangouts and cohorts divided
by even and odd days
into a checkerboard calendar
of camaraderie and loneliness.

Stiff as the drinks
my mother no longer pours
after finding religion
in my brother's ashtray:
Jesus' bearded visage
radiating from a nicotine-
stained Styrofoam plate.

Pockmarked as the sixth moon of Jupiter
after a mining conglomerate
ceases gouging its smooth surface,
hauling an armada of icebergs
through the solar system.

Sure-fire as taking your six-year-old
to see *The Exorcist* and,
in the middle of the night
laying green vomity goo
by the bed until he awakens,
terrified, a livewire bundle
of future therapy bills
and sleep deprivation.

What Rises to the Top

Where has the small goose gone, the one with
the black marked head?
               As if dribbled tar dried
on its tufted crown or a child scrawled joined
circles with a Sharpie, colouring them in: a lop-
sided flower, a rare orchid.
               Another goose—
mean, grey, moulting—eyes me as though
it still had eggs to protect. Hisses.
               Reminds me
of the Irish wolfhound that was left behind
at my friend's new house.
The same disregard for sleekness.
               Too big
to take to an apartment—back level with the
kitchen counter—he was abandoned. For two
weeks drinking stagnant pond water, thick with
scum, and lunging at ducklings and slow
squirrels.
               The dog dead a month later. Everyone
suspected something in the water. I can't even
remember its name.
               And this big goose, patrolling,
manic with power, shakes its indignant head
at me.
               The one I miss—the small one with the black
splotch—gone.

A Foley Artist's Wet Dream

A tinkerbell truck
flits through the intersection,
its trailer-hitch chain
dragging along asphalt.

Half the ghost of Marley
jangling and clanking,
half *When a bell rings,*
an angel gets its wings.

Imagine the tarnished truck
driving to the bottle depot
or the dump, wafting charmed music
through a park no one plays in,

turning heads and sparking
the smiles of workers
who've layered up—t-shirts
and sweaters, jackets, but not gloves,

not yet—who need
to surrender to a flight of fancy
that's melded to the chassis of a beat-up
pickup chiming through the city.

Four Seasons on the Bus: Winter

Old man winter's gone
on a bender. Mumbles
like a tailor whose mouth
is stationed with pin-sentries.

He's announcing, always
in this city, he's announcing
his presence. That his eyes
are going not dim
but effervescent

so that the particles of falling
snow twinkle like full-lustre
diamonds, catching light,

splitting it—he can almost hear
them refract, sounds
like cupboard-warm whisky
poured over two ice cubes.

Must go to the eye doctor,
get his optic nerve
checked out. Must
get sorted at the bank.
Needs a notarized cheque
for his damned lawyer.

She's always blotto,
he says. *Can't trust her
at all.*

His hands, too small,
clench over a belly
that's more last-act Falstaff
than Bacchus. Plumped
sour with regret,
pickled, betrayed, but still
sparring, stabbing,

spieling an absurd
malty gale that can't
really be helped,
just got through,

though the camo-clad
not-so-young men try,
scattering salt and grit
to calm his drunken-
palsy, to staunch his
elemental wounds.

December Scene

Near the rough path behind the strip mall
the fields grow wild:

weed stalks dried and tawny,
not yet weighed down.

Everything coated in hoarfrost.

At the point
where dew would drop,
it gathers.

Too cold for flakes, but minute crystals
catch in the sun
and don't seem to fall.

As if a child upended a shaker of sparkles
she was not supposed to touch
and, worried about being caught,
shut her eyes:

the glare of her blunder
emblazoning
the insides of her lids.

Reading Erin Mouré Midflight or How Capitalism Ends

When the woman in 17-B begins painting her fingernails,
I forget we've given birth to each other's houses:
even the rooms doused with colours
we'd never choose ourselves.

Rooms strong-armed by Doric candlesticks, would-be
murder weapons posited two to a table,
within grasp.

And in drawers, overlooked
safety pins, now fused to the particleboard
through their own rusting, can no longer
hold split seams or themselves together.

The whalebone corsets of bathroom wallpaper
laced so tight that the water pipes clamp off
and the air-intake grates jam with collapsed plaster,
and the doors and the windows seize shut,
and the medicine cabinets slip their moorings: broken
bottles, chemicals bathing the chequered tiles.

This miasmic claustrophobia that we all gift
one another.

After the flight attendant sniffs her out
and insists the woman stop her preening,
she looks up with a who, me expression—
which is the closest to innocence adults have
at 30,000 feet—like a shopper caught denting

honeydew after honeydew checking for a degree
of ripeness that doesn't exist.

Finally, she stops up
the amethyst-hued bottle, beholds
her half-done hands. The smell doesn't
dissipate: it darts about like a keyed-up
toddler as we go nose dumb,
keeling into our toluene-laden descent.

News-scroll for Dream Junkies

>>>Somebody's going to break a leg, but it won't be me>>>The dry-rot walkway softens like a stale cookie forgotten atop the fridge>>>To be chic, remove an item before leaving the house>>>Fashion advice for southerners like Coco Chanel who didn't winter in Winnipeg where the wind is the Wendigo that hates you>>>A conundrum: needing to bring along what you cannot pack>>>Even memories end up on the no-fly list>>>A scholar slips herself between the pages of a book and is lost>>>Yes, I have sluiced through the needle's eye like I was greased with purpose>>>Call it a caffeine addiction or a sense of my own limitations>>>Never mind the crows squawking in the fleeced trees or the moon's still visible, faint persistence, like the throb after a hangnail's pulled>>>Richard III was killed by two blows to his bare head, his cracked cranium, a headline that snuck up on him, one he'll never read>>>In dreams when I fly, it's the power lines that strike fear>>>Is there a difference between *soar* and *sore?*>>>Don't play with your wounds: they're pink and healthy as watermelons>>>And forget about flying's evil twin, for your children will dream of porches>>>

Wilde Paints the Parlour White

Why I have seen wallpaper which must lead a boy brought up under its influence to a career of crime.
—OSCAR WILDE, 1882, Fredericton

Oscar dons a dark blue smock,
grabs a paintbrush, streaks
a coarse wall with white paint—

a hint of grey in the undertone,
like an Arctic hare,
or a dress-shirt
washed with too little bleach.

He ends with a flourish,
not camp, but poised—
signs his name, white on white—
catches a solitary drip in his palm.

Days later Oscar unlatches a trunk.
With a magician's sense
he draws yards of textiles
from its cavity:

thick weaves, subtle variations
of green and ores.

Oscar drapes the folds
over the length of his
outstretched arms.
A luxurious Messiah.

He moves to the couch,
lays the fabric out like a sick
child to rest. Picks one, then another,
holds each against the virgin wall,
plays with the wooden shutters—
just the right amount of light.

He calls for a hammer, nails.
Calls for someone to clear the couch;

he's chosen the palest of greens,
as if celery had breath,
and a matte gold, the shade
of exhumed antiques.

Oscar drapes
and thinks of lamps.

In the Torso of a Great Windstorm
Odds and Ends, 1939

> *The wind makes everything alive…*
> *Without movement a subject is dead. Just look!*
> —SUSAN VREELAND imagining Emily Carr in *The Forest Lover*

Put your head over a flashlight,
watch it glow faerie pink. Picture—
lit from inside—a belly torch,

the backdrop—
knot of spruce tree organs: liver, kidneys,
        bundle of intestine, stomach—
                cool blue and green foliage hiding enzymes,
                bacterium, acids.

That exact texture of pulse,
        quiver, musculature connected
        and contained, skyline and dirt grouted
        together, a vista of
                    inner skin, the underside.
                    Airstream gale whipping
                            the pinprick stars into dashes,
                        molars into canines, evolution
        of the Spartan firmaments. A breezy muse,
        that gust of inspiration.

Now look at the actors erect at centre stage, see:
        skinny veins with plump tops,
                or—zooming in—synapses of birch foregrounded.
Holy trifecta
announcing skyward:
        home, joy, hunger.

How to Live in the Belly of a Blue Whale

Getting to the belly's a challenge.
Despite how large a mass of mammal,
she's got a throat the diameter of a grapefruit.
She'll no more swallow you whole
than lace up skates for a game of shinny.

So hire a team of divers, anaesthesiologists,
surgeons, cauterizers, and slip
through the entry wound. Recognize
that this is some kind of backwards birth:
a flesh tunnel into a body buoyant.

A glass suit will protect you
from gastric juices, though what you see
will be distorted. You must regard your sight's
askew nature as a gift: voyagers and artists
never quite see straight.

Take notes, pictures. Document everything.
If you fail to provide ample proof,
listeners will give your tale the misnomer of *fishy*.

Remember the warm-blooded connection.
Remember fins as legs, blowhole as nostril.
Remember skin basking in sunlight.

Most important, have your escape route planned;
although Geppetto packed
matches and wooden furniture,

you'd be better served
carting stimulant laxative,
an industrial dose.

That your expulsion happens near the surface
is a blessing.

During your first public address
acknowledge your predecessors:
van Valkenborch's painting should do the trick,
and don't forget Geppetto, your spirit-
guide, that moustachioed bachelor will lead you
far enough away from sense that you'll
be a comrade to both sages and plankton,
children and evolutionists.

And each and every night, beseech Jonah
to protect you from bad whale-gut dreams:
the mattress beneath you swelling and shunting,
and a heart the weight of a compact car,
its beat clocking you about the head.

Two Ways to Stay Dry

I

Leaving the sedan,
the boy grasps his mother's hand,
attempts to bound
a sewer grate

but hits the slush-edge
with a splatter.

Gumboots, black
rubber sheen up to the ankles
where the melt reaches,

white-etched salt stains
above that high-water
mark.

His mother pulls him safe
into the pharmacy,
avoids drips from awnings.

II

In front of a posh café,
a homeless man
dons dingy running shoes,
grey and losing shape,

and instead of socks, his pant cuffs
tuck into mismatched grocery bags,
bulges of wrinkled plastic
tied tight around his calves.

He's carted a crate street-side,
studied the rain gutters,
scoped out the corners where
the cars swell and heave slurry puddles.
And has taken his place.

An Aerie, All Winter

On the train bridge, between the metal joints,
bald eagles build mammoth aeries,
and in the northside oaks,
broad crooks hold mud-caked, twiggy bowls:
slapdash marvels of engineering.

All winter, these feathered dinosaurs
snag and scoop outdoor cats. Seize squirrels:
drab blotches desperate to find
their mislaid stockpiles.

No mistake, the haste of predator-shadow
on blanched ice-jams does impress,
but for me, it's really these nests;
if I had hollow bones, I'd crawl in,

bed down 'til spring,
wake up surrounded by buds,
looking for the south-flyers returning to feed
on yielding ground, hungry too.

Maunderings

I can't go on like this aware
of monster throats beneath the street I'm losing
my centrality
——DON MCKAY

The choice of pigeon as pace horse makes your gait eccentric.
Everything falls at Dutch angles.

Ice white-washing the window; cataract deglinted by overcast.
Sketch here a Venn diagram of my potential losses.

Wicker split and working loose: a chair left street-side,
tinder for delinquent blaze, tomorrow's charred curb.

Read to me a choked passage.
Are you beyond, slim column, cavern-stuck in a maze-cave?

Sew a casein button, a milky aperture, back on an old cardigan.
Feel the frayed sleeve, the pilled wool.

Against metal beams the Saint John current chafes its chilblains,
grinds ice down to manageable shards.

Here's a weald—rich, damp—that we get lost in far too often.
Let's pad past the cemetery: don't ever trust the dead.

At the kitchen table, granddad rolls his own smoke,
his slug tongue secreting a glue trail.

Last year June bugs collided against the hatchback windshield.
The year before cicadas abraded the afternoons with their song.

You dress with practice, know to distrust warm-bloodedness.
Don't bargain with the elements. Try your hand at constant worry.

The sun is a cigarette tip smouldering through gauze.
A bald-eagle iris loosening fog, tulle to talon.

In your mother's top drawer is the birthplace of nostalgia.
Yellowed paper towel swaddling an old tooth, dried blood on its root.

In a town of skunks, even the trees have turned.
Post-blizzard, smeared on each one, a hoary vertical stripe.

History hones on its ruthless whetstone.
Budgeting guilt is easier than budgeting contentment.

Then the gun-clap of fabric yanked taut.
The kickback of certain consonants.

The church bells hollow out the dawn.
An augury of pigeons noiselessly gorge and circle.

Meanings are devilish playthings:
a chipped tooth, a grimy puddle for jumping over.

Graffiti on the 18th-century brickwork.
Quebec Libre! scrawled over patchwork Fleur de lis. *Moi Moi Moi*
stamped in a metal door.

Your friend's grandfather clock stops working.
A stilled scythe in a museum case.

Three right turns and you're speeding eastward again.
The sun resolute as a gobstopper stuck in your throat.

Harp strings and hatpins.
We built our days upon near intangibles.

My kettle screams like a concert-mad teenybopper.
Adolescent heat steaming the cupboard bottoms out of shape.

Tomorrow you'll smoke-drowse the wasp nest, grey as a cigarette-
      pack lung.
Each gust could bring the whole angry lot down.

Stop me if you've not heard this one.
It helps if you hum along, if you keep the beat with your breath.

The jean-clad man in the back pew is crying;
the shrewd congregation strains not to hear.

Collar bone scything through unlined black lace.
That graceful friend who won't forgive you.

As sheet lightning peroxides the neighbourhood into alienscape,
you tally static strikes bursting from the AM radio.

The birch trees' fawn-hued under-bark is a warning.
Not just white strips peeled for lazy blaze. But signposts. Famine bread.

Dad guts a fresh-caught trout in the driveway.
Blood tendrils on tarmac, hose casting pink mist into humid dusk.

Once you dreamt of being alive without overgrowth.
A perfect ripe plumpness, a figgy balance.

With a woodsman for a father, you memorize the Latinate name of plants.
But he's less impressed when you recite Roethke.

Language has failed you.
There's no word for the feeling of wearing a new hat, catching reflections
        of your bare face framed.

Eyeliner shavings in the bottom of a makeup bag.
Bobby pins. Fine powder on the bathroom mirror.

At times your heart demands brutalist architecture.
At times you hate domes.

The padded snow underfoot, pure compression, is the sharpest thing.
That you once had a shortcut. That you once had time not to waste.

NOTES

The opening epigraph is from Tammy Armstrong's poem "Azimuth" in *Take Us Quietly* published by Goose Lane Editions, 2006.

In "The Observer Effect," the epigraph is from Dennis Coon and John O. Mitterer's *Psychology: A Journey* published by Wadsworth, 2014.

In "Keeping Track, Keeping Pace," the Muybridge sequence is a series of photographs taken by Eadweard Muybridge that revealed the precise movement of galloping horses.

In "Apollo in a Sulky," a sulky is the lightweight cart the driver sits in for harness racing.

"Reading Alden Nowlan's 'Hens' at the Laundromat" is inspired by Nowlan's "Hens" from *Alden Nowlan: Selected Poems*, edited by Patrick Lane and Lorna Crozier, published by House of Anansi Press, 1996.

In "Street Haunting," the epigraph is from Frank O'Hara's "Personal Poem" from *Lunch Poems*, published by City Light Books, 1964. The poem takes its title from Virginia Woolf's essay "Street Haunting," which it also quotes. Although, the actual line is "Let us choose the pearls, for example, and then imagine how, if we put them on, life would be changed." The essay can be found in *The Virginia Woolf Reader*, edited by Mitchell Alexander Leaska, published by Harcourt Brace Janovich, 1984.

In "Peony," the epigraph is from Arthur Rimbaud's "Phrases." The translation is by Wallace Fowlie from *Rimbaud: Complete Works, Selected Letters*, published by the University of Chicago Press, 1996.

In "Vultures over Cottage Country," the epigraph is from Louise Bogan's poem "I Saw Eternity" from *The Blue Estuaries: Poems, 1923–1968*, published by Farrar, Straus and Giroux, 1968.

"How to Survive a Bear Attack" is a found poem inspired by an October 12, 2013 CBC news story: "Man grabs bear's tongue during attack near Grand Falls."

In "Sole-worn Glass," the epigraph is from Catherine Greenwood's "Silver-Haired Bat Caught in a Ceiling Lamp" from *The Lost Letters*, published by Brick Books, 2013.

"curb' N.— " is a definition poem based on Jeramy Dodds's poem "RAC*COON' N.—" from *Crabwise to the Hounds*, published by Coach House Books, 2008.

In "Shield Lichen," the Latin name for the title lichen is Parmelia sulcata.

In "Similes from Pure Sleep," the epigraph is from Yvonne Harrison and James Horne's article, "Sleep loss impairs short and novel language tasks having a prefrontal focus" from the *Journal of Sleep Research*.

In "What Rises to the Top," the first line is inspired by a line in an untitled poem from Frank O'Hara's book *Lunch Poems* published by City Light Books, 1964. O'Hara's line is "Where had the swan gone, the one with the lame back?"

In "Reading Erin Mouré Midflight or How Capitalism Ends," the book being read is Erin Mouré's *WSW (West South West)* published by Véhicule Press, 1989. From the book, I also quote from a poem, "Excess": "We have given birth to each other's homes."

"Wilde Paints the Parlour White" takes liberty with Oscar Wilde's visit to Fredericton in 1882. There he gave a speech titled "The House Beautiful," which was about the importance of aesthetics in interior design.

In "In the Torso of a Great Windstorm," the epigraph is from *The Forest Lover*, a novel written in the voice of Emily Carr by Susan Vreeland, published by Viking, 2004.

"How to Live in the Belly of a Blue Whale" references the sixteenth-century painting "Jonah and the Whale" by Frederik van Valkenborch. In the painting, the whale is, as is described in the book of Jonah in the *King James Bible*, "a great fish."

In "Maunderings," the epigraph is from Don McKay's poem "Lependu Flu," which can be found in *Angular Conformity*, published by Goose Lane Editions, 2014.

ACKNOWLEDGEMENTS

Thank you to the editors of the following journals for publishing poems from this book: *Exile: The Literary Quarterly*, *The Malahat Review*, *QWERTY Magazine*, *FreeFall Magazine*, *CV2*, *Prairie Fire*, *EVENT*, *Grain Magazine*, *The Puritan*, and *The Fiddlehead*.

Thank you to artsnb, who provided me with a grant that allowed for the completion of this book.

"In the torso of a great windstorm," "We Met Midway Up the Hill," and "Shield Lichen" were previously published in the chapbook *Maunder* (Frog Hollow Press, 2015). Greatest thanks to Shane Neilson and Caryl Peters who craft gorgeous books, inside and out.

Thanks to everyone at Palimpsest!!!

Thanks to the following people who helped me with drafts of these poems: Anne Compton, Brittany Lauton, Ian LeTourneau, Jeramy Dodds, John Barton, Kayla Geitzer, Leah Schoenmakers, Martin Ainsley, Michael Jessome, Mike Meagher, Nick Thran, Rebecca Salazar, Ross Leckie, and Sue Sinclair.

To my first reader and love, Rob Ross. Thanks for helping me push myself and for reeling me in when I've taken things too far.

To my Mum, who has a curiosity and humour about the world that taught me everything important.

AUTHOR BIOGRAPHY

Claire Kelly's work has been published in various literary journals, including *The Malahat Review, Exile Quarterly, Event,* and *Prism International.* Her chapbook, *Ur-Moth,* was published in 2014 by Frog Hollow Press. *Maunder* is her first full-length collection. She lives and writes in Edmonton, Alberta.

Author photo by MATT QUIRING PHOTOGRAPHY